Pond Life to Spot

Illustrated by
Stephanie Fizer Coleman

Designed by Lenka Hrehova and Jenny Brown
Words by Kate Nolan

As you look through this book, you will see that months are given in the descriptions of some plants and animals. These show the time of year when you are most likely to see them. If no months are mentioned, they can be spotted all year round.

D1312860

Fishes

Look for its red fins and tail

Perch

You might spot some of these fish swimming together in a group (or shoal). They like clean, shaded water.

Three-spined stickleback

A small but aggressive hunter, with three sharp spines on its back, and silvery scales on its sides and belly.

Thick, slimy, slippery skin

Tench

Usually hides among weeds at the bottom of lakes and slow-flowing rivers, or lies buried in the mud.

Minnow

Watch for large shoals
of these tiny fish in clear,
flowing water such as
streams and rivers.

Carp

Likes to bask in the sun near
the surface of weed-filled lakes.
Look for the whisker-like
barbels (feelers) near
its mouth.

Pike

This fast, fierce hunter lurks
in dense weed. It uses its huge
jaws to catch fish, frogs, small
mammals and even water birds.

Can be over
a metre long

Amphibians and reptiles

Lays eggs in ponds in spring

Common frog

Its smooth green or brown skin can become lighter or darker for camouflage. February-October.

Grass snake

Often seen swimming in ponds, or sunbathing nearby. It does not bite or harm humans. April-October.

Smooth newt

Look for it in cool, damp places, such as under logs. March-October.

Great crested newt

This large newt has rough, knobbly skin, with black spots on its orange belly. March-October.

Males have a wavy crest in spring

Warty, green-brown skin

Common toad

Wide and stocky, with copper-coloured eyes. Hunts slugs and snails at night. February-October.

Palmate newt

In spring, you might spot it visiting ponds on heaths or moors to lay its eggs. March-October.

5

Flying insects

Emperor dragonfly

Look out for this large blue and green insect flying high above water in summer. June-August.

Lays eggs in floating pondweed

Stonefly

Rests on rocks and trees near water, with its dark grey-brown wings folded flat over its body. April-June.

Has two thick tail bristles

Clear, lacy wings

Mayfly

A delicate insect with three long, thin tail bristles. Flies in swarms just above the water's surface. April-September.

Caddis fly

Looks like a moth with hairy wings

You might spot this insect flying near water at dusk. February-November.

Common blue damselfly

Often visits garden ponds. Bright turquoise-blue body with black markings. April-September.

Common darter

Small and slender. It hovers in the air, and then darts forward to catch other insects. July-October.

Bugs and beetles

Backswimmer

You might spot it swimming jerkily, usually on its back. Traps bubbles of air on its body to breathe underwater.

Uses back legs like paddles

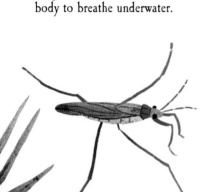

Pond skater

Skims across the surface of still or slow-moving water, using its front legs to scoop up insects to eat. April-October.

Whirligig beetle

Watch for large groups of these beetles swimming rapidly in circles on the water's surface.

Has two pairs of eyes to see above and below the water

Water measurer

Look at the edges of ponds, slow rivers and streams. It uses vibrations in the water to track down its insect prey.

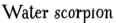

Holds an air bubble to let it breathe underwater

Saucer bug

Uses its sharp beak to stab smaller creatures at the bottom of weed-filled, muddy ponds.

Water scorpion

Hides among plants in shallow water. Its 'tail' is a long tube, used for breathing underwater like a snorkel.

Under the surface

Water spider

Builds its bell-shaped web between plant stems under the water, then fills the web with bubbles of air to breathe.

Great diving beetle

Dives down to the bottom of ponds to hunt for insects, small fish and even frogs. It stores air under its wing cases to breathe underwater.

Great pond snail

Watch for this large snail crawling over water plants.

Horse leech

You might see leeches
clinging to stones or plants,
or swimming with a rippling motion.

Has a long snorkel-like tube
for breathing underwater

Water stick insect

Look in shallow water, where
it waits among reeds and stems
for tadpoles and other prey.

Water louse

Related to the woodlouse,
this insect hides under
stones in ponds, eating
rotting plants.

Mammals

Daubenton's bat

Flies fast and low over the
water's surface hunting for
insects. April-October.

Endangered in Britain

Water vole

Has small ears and a furry
tail. Watch for its rounded
nose showing above the
water as it swims along.

Otter

Large, strong swimmer with
webbed feet. Rare and hard to
spot. Look around clean rivers
with lots of fish and plant life.

*Can close ears and
nose underwater*

Beaver

Has webbed feet and a scaly, flat tail. Became extinct in Britain about 400 years ago, but has been brought back. It is still very rare.

Uses mud and sticks to build dams

Common pipistrelle

Darts through the air over parks and wetlands, eating up to 3,000 flying insects in a single night. April-October.

Water shrew

Dense, velvety fur and a pointed nose. Swims very well underwater, where it hunts insects and small fish.

13

Birds

Moorhen

Easy to spot on ponds, lakes and rivers. It has a bright red beak with a yellow tip, and yellow legs.

Little grebe

Look out for the fluffy feathers on its rear end as it dives down to catch fish and insects.

Spends nearly all of its life on the water

Grey heron

Stands completely still at the edges of ponds and canals, waiting to catch fish with its sharp beak.

Wigeon

You might see large flocks of these birds on wetlands in winter, searching for plants and seeds in shallow waters.

Look for its round head and short beak

Coot

Look for the white 'shield' above its beak. It ducks down into deeper water to catch insects.

Mallard

Britain's most common duck. Male mallards have yellow beaks, and shiny, green feathers covering their heads.

Waterside plants

Water forget-me-not

Its tiny, pale blue flowers have yellow middles, and grow on arching stems. June-September.

Greater pond sedge

Grows in clumps of tall stems, with spiked brown flowers and bright green leaves. June-September.

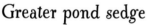

Osier willow

This tree has long, thin, leaves and smooth, flexible branches. In spring, it grows greenish-yellow catkins.

Common alder

Its cone-like fruits drop seeds into rivers to help spread them. You might see its roots growing from riverbanks into the water.

Devil's-bit scabious

Watch for butterflies and bees visiting its rounded, purplish-blue flowers. July-October.

Great willowherb

Tall, with hairy leaves and stems. Look for its deep pink flowers with cream middles. June-September.

Shallow~water plants

Yellow flag iris

Its large, bright yellow flowers
with drooping petals grow on
tall stems. Found in marshes
or on riverbanks. May-August.

Great reedmace

Has long, pointed leaves. Dark brown,
velvety seedheads develop at the ends
of its spiky stems. June-August.

Creeping Jenny

Grows low down, 'creeping' along
the ground in shady, damp places.
Look for its rounded leaves and
yellow flowers. May-August.

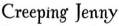

Water plantain

Large, pointed, oval leaves. Its small, purplish-pink flowers each have three petals. June-September.

Its pretty flowers can be pink or pale lilac

Water mint

The leaves of this plant give off a strong, minty smell when they're crushed. July-October.

Common reed

You might see this plant's tall stems with fluffy flower spikes growing in bushy 'beds' at the water's edge. August-October.

Plants in the water

Frogbit

Rises to the water's surface in spring. Shiny, round leaves, and white flowers with thin, crumpled petals. July-August.

Watercress

Thick blankets of leaves float on the surface of clean, shallow water. May-October.

Look for its small white and green flowers

Water crowfoot

Its white flowers with yellow middles each have five petals. Look for it in ponds, streams and ditches. May-September.

White water-lily

Its large white flowers and flat, rounded leaves (sometimes called 'lily pads') float on ponds and canals. June-August.

Spiked water-milfoil

Its brush-like leaves drift beneath the water, and small red flowers grow on tall stems above it. June-July.

Tiny flowers in spring

Curled pondweed

Its long, leathery leaves have wavy edges, and float beneath the surface of the water. May-October.

21

Spotting chart

Once you've spotted some pond life from this book, find its sticker at the back, and stick it on this chart in the space below its name.

Backswimmer	Beaver	Caddis fly	Carp	Common alder
Common blue damselfly	Common darter	Common frog	Common pipistrelle	Common reed
Common toad	Coot	Creeping Jenny	Curled pondweed	Daubenton's bat
Devil's-bit scabious	Emperor dragonfly	Frogbit	Grass snake	Great crested newt
Great diving beetle	Great pond snail	Great reedmace	Great willowherb	Greater pond sedge

Grey heron	Horse leech	Little grebe	Mallard	Mayfly
Minnow	Moorhen	Osier willow	Otter	Palmate newt
Perch	Pike	Pond skater	Saucer bug	Smooth newt
Spiked water-milfoil	Stonefly	Tench	Three-spined stickleback	Water crowfoot
Water forget-me-not	Water louse	Water measurer	Water mint	Water plantain
Water scorpion	Water shrew	Water spider	Water stick insect	Water vole
Watercress	Whirligig beetle	White water-lily	Wigeon	Yellow flag iris

Index

First published in 2021 by Usborne Publishing Ltd., Usborne House, 83-85 Saffron Hill, London EC1N 8RT, England.
usborne.com Copyright © 2021 Usborne Publishing Ltd. The name Usborne and the Balloon logo are trade marks
of Usborne Publishing Ltd. All rights reserved. No part of this publication may be reproduced, stored in a
retrieval system or transmitted in any form or by any means, electronic, mechanical, photocopying,
recording or otherwise without the prior permission of the publisher. Printed in China. UKE.

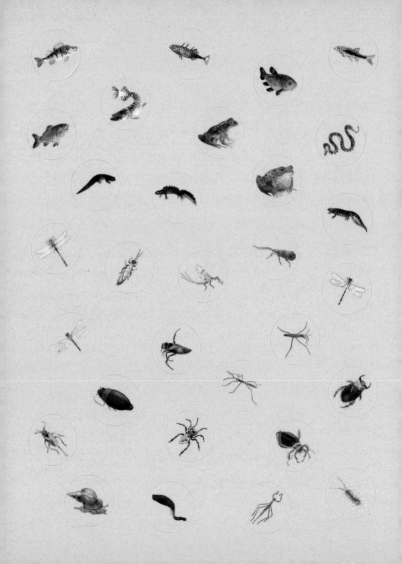